Vegan Thai

Over 35 Vegan Thai Food Recipes That BEAT Any Takeout

By

Katya Johannsson

Copyright © 2016

All rights reserved

« Introduction »

According to Wikipedia's definition of Thai cuisine we learn that: "Every country in the world has its own food profile. It reflects its culture, environment, ingenuity and values. In the case of Thailand, these words come to mind: intricacy; attention to detail; texture; color; taste; and the use of ingredients with medicinal benefits, as well as good flavor".

Thailand was known as Siam in the past. Chinese influences on Thai cooking included the use of noodles, dumplings, soy sauce, and other soy products. Like the Chinese, the Thais based their recipes on blending five basic flavors: salty, sweet, sour, bitter, and hot.

Rice is the main dietary ingredient of Thailand. Thais eat two kinds of rice: the standard white kind and glutinous, or sticky, rice. Rice is also used in desserts very often. Rice is eaten at almost every meal and also made into flour used in noodles, dumplings, and desserts.

Thai seasoning is hot and spicy and common flavorings are fish sauce, dried shrimp paste, lemon grass, coriander, basil, garlic, ginger, cumin, cardamom, and cinnamon.

Coconuts play an important role in the Thai diet. Coconut milk and shredded coconut are used in many dishes, especially desserts

Thais do not use chopsticks unless they are eating noodles

Contents

1. Salt & Pepper Tofu

Ingredients:

- ½ cup cornstarch
- 1 tsp salt
- ½ tsp pepper
- 1 tsp garlic powder
- 1 tsp Ener-G Egg Replacer
- 2 tbsp. water
- 1 lemon
- 1 pound silken extra firm tofu*, cut into triangles or small rectangles
- 1 red bell pepper (capsicum), cut into long strips
- 1 large white onion, sliced
- 1 green onion, chopped
- 1 bunch fresh coriander (cilantro), chopped
- Vegetable oil, for frying

Method:

1. In a medium-sized bowl, mix the cornstarch, salt, pepper and garlic powder.
2. In another bowl, mix the vegan egg, water and juice of ½ the lemon.
3. Dip the tofu in the vegan egg mixture and then into the cornstarch mixture.
4. Set on a plate and set aside.
5. Heat 1 tbsp. of oil in a frying pan over medium-high heat.
6. Sauté the red bell pepper, white and green onions until cooked but still crunchy.
7. While the veggies are cooking, heat 2 tbsp. of oil over medium-high heat in another frying pan.
8. Fry tofu until golden brown on both sides.

9. Divide the veggies onto 2 plates, top with tofu and sprinkle generously with cilantro.
10. Serve with lemon wedges.

2. Red Curry Quinoa

Ingredients:

- 1 cup quinoa
- 1 (400ml) can coconut milk
- ¾ cup vegetable broth (or water)
- 2-3 tbsp. vegan red curry paste (see note)
- 2 tbsp. raw sugar (or brown sugar)
- 1 tbsp. Sriracha sauce or 1 tsp crushed red chili pepper
- 1 tsp coconut or vegetable oil
- 1 clove garlic, minced
- 3 cups colorful veggies (onions, carrots, red bell pepper, broccoli, etc.)
- Fresh basil and/or cilantro

Method:

1. In a medium saucepan, mix quinoa, coconut milk, vegetable broth, red curries paste, sugar, and Sriracha sauce or red chili flakes.
2. Bring to boil, then lower heat to lowest setting and cover saucepan.
3. Simmer until the quinoa is ready, about 15 minutes. If the liquid is almost all absorbed but the quinoa is still not ready, stir another ¼ cup of water in.
4. While quinoa is cooking, heat oil over medium heat and stir-fry the garlic and veggies.
5. Mix veggies with quinoa and serve, garnished with fresh basil and cilantro.

3. Green Curry Noodle Bowl

Ingredients:

- 1 tbsp. unrefined coconut oil
- 1/2 red onion, diced
- 2 cloves of garlic, minced
- 1-inch chunk fresh ginger, minced
- 1 red bell pepper, diced
- Handful frozen green peas
- Handful shelled edamame
- 1 1/2 cup veggie broth
- 1 cup coconut milk
- 2 serving thin rice noodles
- 2 tablespoons green curry paste
- 1 tbsp. rice vinegar
- Juice of one lime
- 1 tbsp. tamari
- Salt and pepper to taste
- Cilantro for garnish

Method:

1. In a medium stockpot set on medium heat, warm the coconut oil.
2. Add the onion, and sauté until nearly translucent (about five minutes).
3. Add the garlic and ginger and sauté for another minute.
4. Add the red bell pepper, green peas, and edamame, and sauté for five minutes.
5. Add vegetable broth, coconut milk, noodles, rice vinegar, lime juice, and tamari.
6. Allow the noodles to simmer in the broth and veggies until they're cooked (between eight and ten minutes.

7. Stir in green curry paste, and add salt and pepper to taste.
8. Garnish with cilantro.

4. Roasted Veggie Thai Curry

Ingredients:

- 1 Sheet Pan of Roasted Veggies from Roasted Market Veggies or
- 1 pound sweet onions, cut into halves then sliced into ¼ half moons
- ½ of a red bell pepper, seeded, sliced into strips then cut into 1cm. rectangles
- ¾ pound of zucchini, cut into quarters lengthwise and sliced crosswise into triangles
- ¾ pound Japanese eggplant, cut into quarters lengthwise and sliced crosswise into triangles
- 3 Tbsp. olive oil
- 1 Tsp. sea salt

Curry:

- 2 Tablespoons Curry paste*, I've used both red & Panang curry paste for this recipe
- 2 Tablespoons avocado oil
- 2 cans - 13.5 ounces each, full fat coconut milk
- 1 Teaspoon sea salt + additional to taste at the end of the cooking time

Method:

1. Roasted veggies already made or you can prepare the veggies and spread them in an even layer on a parchment lined baking sheet.
2. Drizzle with olive oil, sea salt, and roast at 425°F for 20-30 minutes, stirring the vegetables twice during the cooking time.

3. Heat a large skillet over medium high heat.
4. Add the curry paste and the avocado oil to the pan and sauté the curry paste for 1-2 minutes, or until it's very fragrant.
5. Add both cans of coconut milk to the pan and bring the curry back to a boil, stirring to incorporate the curry paste.
6. Lower the heat to medium and simmer the curry for 5-10 minutes - or until the liquid is reduced by ½.
7. Add the roasted veggies to the pan, and simmer for a few minutes to heat up the veggies.
8. Taste the curry and add more salt if necessary.
9. Serve hot with rice, cauliflower rice, rice noodles, or zucchini noodles.

5. Thai Red Curry with Vegetables

Ingredients:

- 1 cup brown jasmine rice or long-grain brown rice, rinsed
- 1 Tbsp. coconut oil or olive oil
- 1 small white onion, diced
- Pinch of salt, more to taste
- 1 Tbsp. finely grated fresh ginger
- 2 cloves garlic, minced
- 1 red bell pepper, sliced into thin 2-inch long strips
- 1 yellow or green bell pepper, sliced into thin 2-inch long strips
- 3 carrots peeled and sliced on the diagonal into ¼-inch wide rounds
- 2 Tbsp. Thai red curry paste
- 1 can full-fat coconut milk
- 1½ cups packed thinly sliced kale (tough ribs removed first)
- 1½ tsp. coconut sugar or brown sugar
- 2 tsp. reduced-sodium soy sauce
- 1½ tsp. rice vinegar
- handful of chopped fresh basil or cilantro
- red pepper flakes
- Sriracha or chili garlic sauce (optional)

Method:

1. To cook the rice, bring a large pot of water to boil.
2. Add the rinsed rice and continue boiling for 30 minutes, reducing heat as necessary to prevent overflow.
3. Remove from heat, drain the rice and return the rice to pot.
4. Cover and let the rice rest for 10 minutes or longer, until you're ready to serve. Just before serving, season the rice to taste with salt and fluff it with a fork.

5. To make the curry, warm a large skillet with deep sides over medium heat. Once it's hot, add a tablespoon of oil.
6. Add the onion and a sprinkle of salt and cook until the onion has softened and is turning translucent, about 5 minutes, stirring often.
7. Add the ginger and garlic and cook until fragrant, about 30 seconds, while stirring continuously.
8. Add the bell peppers and carrots and cook for until they are fork-tender, 3 to 5 more minutes, stirring occasionally.
9. Then add the curry paste and cook, stirring often, for 2 minutes.
10. Add the coconut milk and kale to the pan along with ¾ cup water and 1½ teaspoons sugar. Bring the mixture to a simmer over medium heat.
11. Reduce heat as necessary to maintain a gentle simmer and cook until the peppers, carrots and kale have softened to your liking, about 5 to 10 minutes.
12. Remove the curry from heat and season with rice vinegar and soy sauce.
13. Add salt to taste.
14. Divide rice and curry into bowls and garnish with chopped cilantro and a sprinkle of red pepper flakes, if you'd like.
15. If you love spicy curries, serve with sriracha or chili garlic sauce on the side.

6. Vegetable and Tofu Pad Thai

Ingredients:

- 8 ounces dried wide, flat rice noodles
- 1/4 cup fresh lime juice, plus lime wedges for serving (3 limes)
- 3 Tbsp. soy sauce or fish sauce
- 1 Tbsp. chili sauce, such as Sriracha
- 1 Tbsp. packed dark-brown sugar
- 2 Tbsp. vegetable oil
- 2 Tbsp. Ener-G Egg Replacer
- 1 package (14 ounces) firm tofu, drained, thinly sliced, and patted dry
- 2 medium carrots, peeled and shredded
- 2 garlic cloves, minced
- 8 scallions, white and green parts separated and thinly sliced
- Coarse salt
- 2 Tbsp. roasted salted peanuts, chopped
- 1/4 cup fresh cilantro leaves

Method:

1. Soak noodles according to package instructions; drain.
2. In a small bowl, whisk together lime juice, soy sauce, chili sauce, and brown sugar.
3. In a large nonstick skillet, heat 1/2 teaspoon oil over medium-high, tilting to coat pan.
4. Add vegan eggs, swirl to coat bottom, and cook until just set, about 1 minute. Transfer vegan eggs to a cutting board, loosely roll up, and cut crosswise into thin strips.
5. Add 4 teaspoons oil to skillet and heat.

6. Add tofu in a single layer and cook until golden brown on both sides, 7 minutes, flipping halfway through.
7. Transfer to cutting board.
8. Add 1 1/2 teaspoons oil, carrots, garlic, and scallion whites to skillet and cook until softened, 5 minutes.
9. Add lime-juice mixture and bring to a simmer.
10. Add noodles and cook, stirring frequently, 1 minute. Add vegan eggs and tofu and gently toss to combine.
11. Season to taste with salt.
12. Divide among 4 plates and top with peanuts, cilantro, and scallion greens.
13. Serve with lime wedges.

7. Vegan Pad Thai

Ingredients:

- 200 G. brown rice fettucine noodles (or flat rice noodles)
- 350 G. medium firm tofu
- 2 tbsp. coconut oil (for frying)
- ½ cup thinly sliced onion
- 1 cup thinly sliced carrots
- 1 cup finely chopped celery
- 2 garlic cloves, minced
- 3 cups broccoli florets
- 3 cups bean sprouts
- 2 tbsp. finely chopped green onion
- 2 tbsp. finely chopped cilantro
- 2 tbsp. finely chopped roasted cashews (or peanuts)

Pad Thai sauce ingredients:

- 10 dates, pitted
- 1 cup water
- 2 tbsp. vegan oyster sauce
- 2 tbsp. rice wine vinegar
- 2 tbsp. soy sauce
- 2 tsp sriracha
- 2 tbsp. lime juice
- 2 tsp. miso paste
- 1 tbsp. sesame oil

Method:

1. Drain the water from the tofu and let it sit in paper towel for 10-15 minutes to get rid of excess moisture. Then cut into cubes.
2. Let dates soak in water for 15 minutes. Drain and rinse dates from soaking water. Then place them in a high-powered blender with the rest of the sauce ingredients.
3. Blend until smooth and set aside.
4. Bring a pot of water to a boil for the noodles. Once the water is at a boil, toss in the noodles and stir occasionally while they cook for about 10 minutes. Cook to al dente, drain, and set aside in a colander.
5. Heat a large pan to medium heat and add 1 tbsp. of coconut oil and cubes of tofu. After 4-5 minutes flip the cubes to another side to crisp. Flip the cubes every 2 minutes to get the rest of the sides golden brown.
6. When the tofu cubes are golden brown all around add ¼ cup of the sauce to the pan and coat the pieces evenly cooking over the heat for another minute. Remove tofu from the pan and set aside. You'll toss tofu into the vegetables and noodles near end of cooking time.
7. In the same pan over medium heat add another 1 tbsp. of oil and the onions, carrots, and celery. Cook for 2-3 minutes stirring frequently. Then add in minced garlic and cook for another 1-2 minutes.
8. Add in broccoli and cook for another 4-5 minutes stirring frequently. Then add in half the amount of sauce remaining, toss to coat all the veggies and cook for another 2-3 minutes.
9. Add in the cooked noodles and remaining sauce, turn the heat down to low, toss to coat everything in sauce, and cook for another 3-4 minutes.
10. Adjust the spice level if needed by adding another 1-2 tsp of sriracha.
11. Serve immediately and top with green onion, cilantro, raw sprouts, and chopped cashews or peanuts.

8. Vegan Pad Thai

Ingredients:

- 8 ounces Pad Thai rice noodles
- 6 tbsp. almond butter
- 1 tbsp. tamarind paste
- 2 tsp. toasted sesame oil, divided
- 3 tbsp. tamari, divided into 2 tablespoons and 1 tablespoon
- 2 tbsp. maple syrup
- 1 1/2 tablespoons sriracha (or to taste)
- 1/4 cup lime juice
- 1/3 cup water
- 1 tbsp. olive oil
- 1 clove garlic, minced
- 1 14- to 16-ounce block of extra firm tofu, drained
- 1 tbsp. grated ginger
- 1 large carrot, cut into thin strips
- 4 green onions, halved lengthwise and cut into 1-inch pieces
- 1 1/2 cups mung bean sprouts
- 1/2 cup cilantro, chopped
- 1/4 cup peanuts, chopped
- Lime slices, for garnish

Method:

1. Cook the Pad Thai noodles according to package instructions.
2. Toss them with a teaspoon of sesame oil to prevent too much sticking, and then allow them to cool.
3. Whisk or blend together the almond butter, tamarind paste, the remaining teaspoon of sesame oil, 2 tablespoons of tamari, maple syrup, sriracha, lime juice, and water. Set aside.

4. Heat the olive oil in a large skillet over medium high heat.
5. Add the tofu and cook until it's browning on each side, splashing it as you go with the remaining tablespoon of tamari.
6. Set tofu aside and reduce heat slightly.
7. Add the garlic and ginger to the skillet and even a little extra oil if needed.
8. Cool till the garlic is fragrant, 1 to 2 minutes.
9. Add the carrots and onions, and cook until the carrots are softened but still crisp.
10. Add the noodles and the tofu to the bowl, along with a cup of the sauce.
11. Stir fry the noodles till they're creamy and warm.
12. Add more sauce as you go along, as needed, so that it's well coated.
13. At the very end, stir in the mung bean sprouts, just until they're warm.
14. Divide the noodles onto four plates.
15. Sprinkle with cilantro and peanuts and garnish with lime.

9. Vegetarian Thai Pineapple Fried Rice

Ingredients:

- ½ cup of non-sticky rice
- 1 tbsp. oil
- ½ to ¾ tbsp. chopped garlic
- 8 to 10 cashews split
- Raisins as desired
- ½ cup spring onions and capsicum / bell peppers
- 1 green chili slit (less spicy variety, avoid if making for kids)
- ¼ to ½ tsp curry powder (optional) (for kids ¼ tsp works good)
- 1 to 1½ tsp soya sauce (prefer organic, naturally brewed)(skip for kids)
- 1 tsp vinegar
- Salt as needed
- 1 cup chopped pineapple chunks (use more or less to suit your taste)
- 1 tbsp. fresh coriander leaves / cilantro (chopped)
- Little bit more oil

Method:

1. Wash and soak rice for a while and cook in about 2.5 cups water till al dente.
2. Drain the rice and cool completely.
3. Heat a pan with oil, fry cashews till lightly golden, add raisins and then garlic.
4. Sauté until it smells good.
5. Add chili, bell peppers, and spring onions.
6. Fry until the peppers are lightly cooked but crunchy.
7. Add soya sauce, vinegar, salt and curry powder if using. Mix well.

8. Add in the pineapple chunks.
9. Sauté the pineapples for about 2 minutes.
10. Add the rice, little oil and then the chopped cilantro.
11. Toss everything well and fry for 2 to 3 minutes.
12. Serve hot or warm.

10. Thai Red Curry with Tofu and Mushrooms

Ingredients:

- 1 small yellow onion
- 2 cloves garlic
- 1 teaspoon grated ginger
- 1 red bell pepper
- 1 cup sliced mushrooms
- 3 tablespoons red curry paste
- 12 oz. light coconut milk
- 1-2 tablespoons soy sauce
- 12 oz. extra firm tofu
- 1-2 Thai chilies
- 1 lime, juice and zest
- 8 basil leaves
- Brown basmati rice, for serving

Method:

1. Start cooking some rice.
2. Finely mince the onion, garlic, and fresh ginger.
3. Add these to a large skillet over medium heat with a splash of water and allow to soften for about 5 minutes, until the onions turn slightly translucent.
4. Add in a sliced red bell pepper and sliced mushrooms, about 3 tablespoons of the red curry paste and stir until the paste is evenly coating the veggies.
5. Add in the coconut milk and soy sauce. Stir for a minute or two until the paste has dissolved into the liquid and everything is looking beautiful.
6. Cut the extra firm tofu into fairly large cubes and use a paper towel to squeeze out some excess water.
7. Toss these into the pan along with the juice and zest of 1 lime and, 1-2 minced red chilies.

8. Finally, allow this to simmer uncovered for at least 15 minutes, until the curry reduces and becomes slightly thicker.
9. Add in a few sliced fresh basil leaves and cook for just another minute.
10. Add some salt or more curry paste if needed.
11. Ladle over the rice and enjoy

.

11. Veggie Thai Curry Soup

Ingredients:

- 1 package thin rice noodles or uncooked angel hair pasta
- 1 tablespoon sesame oil
- 2 tablespoons red curry paste
- 1 cup light coconut milk
- 1 carton reduced-sodium vegetable broth
- 1 tablespoon reduced-sodium soy sauce
- 1 package firm tofu, drained and cubed
- 1 can whole baby corn, drained and cut in half
- 1 can bamboo shoots, drained
- 1-1/2 cups sliced fresh shiitake mushrooms
- 1/2 medium sweet red pepper, cut into thin strips
- Fresh basil leaves and lime wedges

Method:

1. Prepare noodles according to package directions.
2. In a stockpot, heat oil over medium heat.
3. Add curry paste; cook 30 seconds or until aromatic.
4. Gradually whisk in coconut milk until blended. Stir in broth and soy sauce; bring to a boil.
5. Add tofu and vegetables to stockpot.
6. Cook 3-5 minutes or until vegetables are crisp-tender.
7. Drain noodles; add to soup and top each serving with basil; serve with lime wedges.

12. Slow Cooker Thai Yellow Curry

Ingredients:

- 1can chickpeas, rinsed and drained
- 1 small orange bell pepper, chopped fine
- 1 medium sweet onion, chopped fine
- 2 medium potatoes, diced into small pieces
- 2 cups crinkle cut carrots or peeled and chopped into ½ inch rounds
- 1 cup frozen peas, thawed
- 1 cup golden raisins
- ¾ cup vegetable broth
- 1 15-ounce can light coconut milk
- 1 tsp garam masala
- ½ tsp cumin
- 1 tsp turmeric
- 1 tsp coriander
- ½ to 1 teaspoon ground sea salt
- 2 tbsp. nutritional yeast
- 1 tbsp. fresh ginger, minced
- 3 garlic cloves, minced
- 1 stalk lemongrass, inner core, chopped

Method:

1. Add all ingredients in slow cooker or crockpot.
2. Cook on low for 8-10 hours or high for 4-6 hours.
3. Serve curry over rice with naan bread.

13. Thai Chickpeas

Ingredient:

- 1 1/2 cups dried chickpeas, picked over and rinsed, soaked overnight in ample water to cover
- 3 cups coconut milk
- 1 tsp. minced garlic
- 3/4 pound sweet potatoes, peeled and cut into 1-inch chunks
- 1 cup coarsely chopped fresh or canned (drained) plum tomatoes
- 1 tbsp. mild curry powder
- 1/4 cup minced fresh coriander
- 1/2 cup minced fresh basil
- 1 to 2 tbsp. tamari soy sauce

Method:

1. Drain and rinse the chickpeas.
2. In the cooker, combine the chickpeas, coconut milk, garlic, sweet potatoes, tomatoes, curry powder, and coriander.
3. Lock the lid in place. Over high heat, bring to high pressure. Lower the heat just enough to maintain high pressure and cook for 18 minutes. Allow the pressure to come down naturally or use a quick-release method. Remove the lid, tilting it away from you to allow any excess steam to escape.
4. If the chickpeas are not tender, return to high pressure for a few more minutes.
5. Add the basil and soy sauce to taste as you break up the sweet potatoes and stir to create a thick sauce.

14. Thai Basil Eggplant

Ingredients:

- 1 large eggplant or 2 medium
- 1 green bell pepper, thinly sliced
- 1 red bell pepper, thinly sliced
- 1 yellow bell pepper, thinly sliced
- 1 white onion, halved and thinly sliced
- 1 14-oz. block firm tofu
- 2 cloves garlic, minced
- Basil leaves
- Vegetable oil
- Hoisin Sauce
- 1/2 cup soy sauce
- 1/4 cup water
- 1-2 tsp chili sauce
- 2 tsp corn starch

Method

1. To Prepare the Eggplant: Cut off the top and bottom tips. Slice the eggplant lengthwise into 3/4-inch slabs. Then cut each slice lengthwise into 3/4-inch slices. Cut each slice into 2 or 3 pieces
2. In a large non-stick pan or stainless steel pan, heat 2-3 tbsp. vegetable oil on medium heat.
3. Add the eggplant pieces and toss to coat them in oil. Add a little amount of water, turn the heat down to low-medium, cover, and let the eggplant cook.
4. Check the eggplant every 5-7 minutes to make sure the eggplant does not burn or stick to the pan. Stir the eggplant pieces and add a little more oil or water to help cook the eggplant and keep it from sticking to the pan. Be sure to add a small amount each time so that the eggplant

will not be watery- mushy. The eggplant is done once it is cooked, but firm so it is still holding shape. Turn off the heat and set aside in the pan.

5. To Prepare the Tofu: cut the tofu block in half. Place each half in a clean paper towel one at a time and squeeze gently to remove excess storage liquid.

6. Cut the tofu into 1/2-Inch cubes and pan fry on medium-high heat with 2 tbsp. vegetable oil, mixing and turning frequently until all the water is burned off and the tofu is lightly golden brown on most sides. Once the tofu is done, set it aside in a separate bowl.

7. To Prepare the Sauce: whisk all ingredients for the sauce. Mix until all the cornstarch has dissolved. Add more chili sauce if you prefer more spice.

8. In the same non-stick frying pan add 1 tbsp. vegetable oil and heat on medium-high.

9. Add the thinly sliced onions and bell peppers. Sauté until they are cooked but still crispy. Add the minced garlic half way through and sauté it into the onions and bell peppers.

10. To Prepare the Dish: add the cooked tofu and veggies to the pan with the cooked eggplant. Turn the heat up to medium and stir in the sauce.

11. Once the pan is hot, turn the heat down to low-medium and mix frequently until the sauce slightly thickens and coats the eggplant and veggies.

12. Turn off the heat and add some freshly chopped basil.

13. Mix once more and serve hot with some quinoa or brown rice.

15. Raw Pad Thai

Ingredients:

- 1 medium zucchini, julienned or spiraled
- 2 large carrots, julienned
- 1 red pepper, thinly sliced
- 1 cup thinly sliced red cabbage
- 3/4 cup frozen edamame, thawed (or try tofu)
- 3 green onions, thinly sliced
- 1 tbsp. hemp seeds
- 1 tsp. sesame seeds

For the dressing:

- •1 garlic clove
- •1/4 cup raw almond butter or peanut butter
- •2 tbsp. fresh lime juice
- •2 tbsp. low-sodium tamari
- •2 tbsp. water
- •2.5 tsp. pure maple syrup (or other sweetener)
- •1/2 tbsp. toasted sesame oil
- •1 tsp freshly grated ginger

Method:

1. Prep vegetables. Add the zucchini, carrots, pepper, and cabbage into one or two large bowls.
2. Toss with hands to combine.
3. Prepare the dressing by processing all dressing ingredients in a mini processor or whisk by hand. The dressing may seem a bit thin at first, but it thickens as it sits.
4. Top bowls with edamame (or tofu), green onion, hemp seeds, and sesame seeds.
5. Pour on dressing and enjoy.

16. Thai sweet potato bean stew

Ingredients:

- 1 large sweet potato, peeled and chopped
- 3 cups cooked kidney beans or chickpeas 2 cans rinsed and drained
- 1 mild jalapeño, seeded and minced
- 1 cup water
- 1 can light coconut milk
- 2 cloves garlic, minced
- 1 tablespoon grated fresh ginger
- 1 cube veggie bouillon
- 1 tbsp. lemon grass, lemon verbena, or lemon balm, minced
- 1/2 tsp. dried ground galangal root (or 1/4 teaspoon coriander plus 1 1/8 tsp. cayenne)
- Zest of 1/2 a lime
- Salt, to taste
- Fresh cilantro

Method:

1. Put everything except the salt and cilantro into a soup pot.
2. Bring to a simmer over medium-high heat and then decrease the heat to low.
3. Cook until the potatoes are easily pierced with a fork, 20 to 30 minutes.
4. Mash a few of the sweet potatoes to thicken up the stew, add salt if needed, and serve over rice.
5. Top with the chopped cilantro.

17. Vegan Tahini Pad Thai

Ingredients:

- 4 cups zucchini, sliced into thin rounds (about 2 large zucchini)
- 4 cups sweet red pepper, sliced into long, thin strips (about 2 large peppers)
- 1 tablespoon olive oil or coconut oil
- 2 garlic cloves, smashed and minced
- ½ tsp. black pepper
- 1 tsp. Celtic sea salt
- 6 tbsp. mild sesame tahini
- 3 tbsp. gluten free tamari
- 1 inch fresh ginger, peeled and minced
- 2 tsp. tamarind powder or paste
- 3 tbsp. fresh lime juice
- 1 tbsp. Sriracha
- 2 tbsp. honey or maple syrup
- 1 tsp black pepper
- ⅓ cup water
- 16 oz. Banh Pho rice noodles
- 1 tbsp. toasted sesame oil
- 1 cup cilantro, chopped

Method:

1. Preheat the oven to 375F. Line a large baking sheet with parchment paper. Set aside.
2. In a large mixing bowl, combine the sliced zucchini and pepper with the olive oil (or coconut oil), minced garlic, black pepper, and salt. Toss to coat the vegetables evenly.
3. Spread the vegetables out on the baking sheet evenly.

4. Roast for 25 - 30 minutes, until the vegetables are fork-tender and beginning to brown or blacken at the edges. Remove from the oven and set aside to cool.
5. Make the sauce: add the tahini, tamari, ginger, tamarind, lime juice, sriracha, honey/maple syrup, black pepper, and water to the bowl of a high powered blender.
6. Blend on high until everything is smooth and creamy. Set aside.
7. Cook the noodles according to package directions. Drain the noodles and rinse in cold water. Drain completely and place the noodles in a large mixing bowl.
8. Add the sesame oil and toss to coat the noodles completely. Put everything together!
9. Add the roasted vegetables to the bowl of noodles along with the sauce and the chopped cilantro.
10. Toss to combine.
11. Serve warm, topped with more cilantro as you like.

18. Thai Zucchini Soup Recipe

Ingredients:

- 2 tbsp. coconut oil
- 1 cup sliced shallots (or onion)
- 1-2 tbsp. green curry paste
- 1 can full fat coconut milk
- 6 medium zucchini, loosely chopped
- 1 cup water, plus more if needed
- Juice of one lime
- Cooked brown rice (or other)

Method:

1. Heat the coconut oil in a large saucepan over medium-high heat, stir in the shallots and a couple generous pinches of salt, and sauté until soft.
2. Stir in the green curry paste along with a dollop of cream from the top of the coconut milk. Stir well, and sauté for another minute or so, until fragrant.
3. Stir in the zucchini with another couple of pinches of salt, and sauté, being careful not to brown, until the zucchini is tender 5-7 minutes.
4. Add the remaining coconut milk and the water, let everything come up to a simmer, and remove from heat.
5. Season the soup with the juice of lime, and salt to taste.
6. Serve over a scoop of brown rice, topped with any of the toppings suggested.

19. Thai Yellow Curry

Ingredients:

- 1 tbsp. rice bran oil
- 1 medium red onion sliced thinly
- 1/4 cup yellow curry paste
- 2 cloves garlic, crushed
- 10 cm. stick fresh lemon grass, bruised
- 4 fresh kaffir lime leaves, shredded finely
- 1 2/3 cups coconut milk
- 1 cup water
- 750 g. orange sweet potatoes, unpeeled, scrubbed, chopped coarsely
- 200 g. green beans, trimmed
- 250 g. assorted mushrooms
- 1 tbsp. finely grated palm sugar
- 1 tbsp. fish sauce (see notes)
- 2 tbsp. lime juice
- 1 fresh long red chili, seeded, sliced thinly
- 1/4 cup fried shallots
- 1/2 cup fresh Thai basil leaves

Method:

1. Heat oil in a wok or large saucepan over high heat; cook onion, stirring, for 5 minutes or until onion softens.
2. Add paste, garlic, lemon grass, and kaffir lime leaves.
3. Cook, stirring, for 1 minute or until fragrant.
4. Add coconut milk, the water and sweet potatoes; bring to the boil.
5. Reduce heat, simmer, uncovered, for 20 minutes or until sweet potatoes are just tender.
6. Stir in beans and mushrooms.

7. Cook, uncovered, for 5 minutes or until vegetables are tender.
8. Stir in sugar, sauce and juice.
9. Remove and discard lemon grass.
10. Serve curry sprinkled with chili, shallots and basil.

20. Squash Pad Thai

Ingredients:

- 1 medium-sized spaghetti squash (about 3-4 pounds)
- 7 tbsp. neutrally-flavored oil, such as canola or vegetable oil
- Sea salt and Freshly ground black pepper
- 4 tbsp. Ener-G Egg Replacer
- 1 (8-ounce) package firm tofu, finely diced (about 1 cup)*
- 1 large red onion, thinly sliced
- 6 cloves garlic, finely minced
- 2 cups carrots, cut into tiny matchsticks
- 2 cups bean sprouts
- 2 bunches scallions, sliced
- 6-8 tbsp. Pad Thai sauce (see below)
- ¾ cup peanuts, chopped
- 1 lime, cut into wedges

Pad Thai Sauce:

- 2 tbsp. light brown sugar
- 2 tbsp. fish sauce
- 2 tbsp. Rice vinegar
- 1 lime, juiced
- 2 tbsp. Tamarind nectar
- 1 clove garlic, minced
- Pinch Red Pepper Flakes

Method:

1. Prepare the Pad Thai Sauce: combine brown sugar, fish sauce, rice vinegar, juice of 1 lime, tamarind nectar, minced garlic, and red pepper flakes (optional) in a small saucepan over medium low heat. Cook sauce, stirring occasionally,

until brown sugar is completely dissolved. It should yield about 8 tablespoons of sauce.

2. Preheat your oven to 400°F. Cut the spaghetti squash in half.
3. Remove seeds and stringy guts, and brush the cut sides of the squash with 1 tablespoon of oil.
4. Season with salt and freshly ground black pepper.
5. Place spaghetti squash, cut side down, on a baking sheet and roast until tender and easily pierced with a knife, about 45-60 minutes. To test if your squash is done, scrap the flesh with a fork. If the strands come off easily, it's done.
6. Let the cooked spaghetti squash cool for about 5 minutes and then scrape all the flesh into a pile of spaghetti strands.
7. Taste and season with some more salt and pepper if needed.
8. Heat 3 tablespoons of oil in a wok or large skillet over high/medium-high heat.
9. Once oil is hot, add tofu and cook, stirring frequently, for 3-4 minutes.
10. Remove tofu and set aside.
11. Add remaining 3 tablespoons of oil to the pan.
12. Add red onions and cook for 1 minute. Add garlic and cook for 1 minute, stirring constantly to avoid burning. Add carrots, bean sprouts, and scallions to pan and cook for 1 minute. Return the cooked tofu to the pan with 6 tablespoons of the Pad Thai sauce and stir.
13. Add the egg substitute and cook until just set.
14. Combine into the Pad Thai mixture.
15. Add cooked spaghetti squash and gently toss everything together and cook for 1-2 minutes.
16. Taste and if Pad Thai needs more flavor, stir in the other 2 tablespoons of sauce.

Serve Pad Thai immediately with lime wedges and chopped peanuts.

21. Thai Tofu Soup

Ingredients:

- 1 cup of egg tofu
- 1 carrot sliced
- 5 Chinese leaves sliced
- 1 vegetable stock cube
- 38g. glass noodles
- 1 tbsp. soy sauce
- chopped spring onion for garnish
- chopped coriander for garnish
- garlic oil for garnish

Method:

1. Bring 1 liter of water to the boil in a pot, and then add 1 vegetable stock cube.
2. Stir until it has dissolved in the water.
3. Add 1 sliced carrot, and let them cook in the broth for about 5 minutes.
4. Add 5 sliced Chinese leaves, and stir. Let the Chinese leaves simmer in the broth for a couple of minutes, then add 38g of glass noodles and 1 cup of egg tofu, and let the soup simmer for about 5 minutes whilst stirring gently so as not to break up the tofu.
5. Add 1 tbsp. of soy sauce, stir, and let the soup simmer for a final 2 to 3 minutes until the glass noodles are cooked. They are ready once they turn clear.
6. Spoon the soup into a bowl, and garnish with chopped spring onion, coriander, and garlic oil.

22. Thai Naan Pizza

Ingredients:

- 2 naan flatbreads
- 2 tbsp. red curry paste
- 3 tbsp. tomato paste
- chopped red onion
- thinly sliced red bell pepper
- grated carrots
- nutritional yeast
- cilantro

Method:

1. Preheat oven to 350F and place naan on baking sheet.
2. Set aside.
3. In small bowl, mix together red curry paste and tomato paste. Using a rubber spatula or spoon, evenly distribute sauce on naan.
4. Top with onion, bell pepper, grated carrots, and nutritional yeast.
5. Garnish with cilantro if desired.
6. Bake pizzas for 15-20 minutes, or until naan has crisped up.
7. Allow pizzas to cool for 5 minutes before slicing and serving.

23. Pad Thai Soup

Ingredients:

- 3 tabs oil
- 2 cloves garlic, minced
- 3 oz. extra firm tofu, diced (or cubed chicken)
- 4 cups broth (veggie or chicken)
- 4 oz. rice noodles (also called pad thai noodles)
- 3 tbsp. soy sauce
- 1/4 tsp sriracha
- 1 tbsp. fish sauce (For vegan, use adaptation listed in above post)
- 1/4 cup roasted peanuts, crushed
- 1/4 cup green onion
- 1 tsp. crushed red peppers

Method:

1. In a large pot, heat the oil.
2. Add the garlic and stir.
3. Add the tofu and cook until lightly fried about 3 minutes.
4. Add the broth, then add the noodles, soy, sriracha, fish sauce, and peanuts.
5. Cook until noodles have softened, about 5 minutes.
6. Serve topped with peanuts, green onions and red chili flakes.

24. Fried Tofu with Peanut Dipping Sauce

Ingredients:

- 1 bag Cubed Deep Fried Tofu

Peanut Dipping Sauce:

- 5-7 sprigs sliced cilantro
- 1 tsp. ground fresh chili paste
- 2 tbsp.   toasted and crushed peanuts
- 1 pinch salt
- 2 tbsp.   sugar
- 2 tbsp.   vinegar

Method:

1. In a microwavable bowl, combine sugar, ground fresh chili paste, salt and vinegar.
2. Heat up for a minute or until sugar is dissolved.
3. Stir the sauce with a spoon to blend all the ingredients in.
4. Add the crushed, toasted peanuts and top with the sliced cilantro.

25. Tapioca Dumplings

Ingredients:

- 2 cilantro
- 2 cilantro roots
- 1 tbsp. fish sauce
- 1/4 - 1/2 teaspoon ground pepper
- 1/2 cup ground spicy tofu
- 1/2 cup onion
- 1/4 cup toasted and ground peanuts
- 1 tbsp. sugar
- 1/2 cup tapioca- small pearl
- 6 - 7 Thai chili pepper
- 1 - 2 tbsp. cooking oil
- 1/2 cup water
- 1 - 2 Green Lettuce

Method:

1. Soak tapioca pearls in room temperature water. The ratio of tapioca to water is one to one. It takes at least 15 minutes to get the tapioca pearl into a workable stage. The tapioca pearls will expand 10%-15%.
2. Wash and keep green lettuce, cilantro, cilantro roots, and fresh Thai chili peppers in water while working on the filling.
3. If you are using raw peanuts, toast the peanuts in the pan (without oil) for 5 minutes or until they're lightly brown. Let the peanuts cool before grinding.
4. Mince garlic, cilantro roots and onion together (picture 3).

5. Cooking the Filling: over medium heat, add 1-2 tablespoons of oil into a pan/wok. Add the minced garlic, cilantro and onion to the pan. Stir until the onion is

translucent. Add the coarsely ground peanuts. Stir to mix everything together. Add sugar, fish sauce and ground pepper. Stir and mix all the ingredients well. The filling should start to turn brownish at this point. If it starts to stick to the bottom of the pan, add a tablespoon of water to release it.

6. The filling should be salty and sweet and seem over seasoned. Well-seasoned filling will be balanced by the bland tapioca wrap. Adjust the seasonings if necessary.

7. Let the filling cool while working on the tapioca wrap.

8. When the filling is cooled enough to handle, make a ball about ½ to ¾ of an inch in diameter. Squeeze the filling tightly into a ball so that it's easier to put into the tapioca wrap. When the filling is completely cooled, it should stick together.

9. Prepare the Steamer: the biggest concern is sticking, so, to prevent the dumplings from sticking, line steamer with shredded banana leaf and oil the banana leaf. Alternatively, you can use parchment paper or just paint the bottom of your steamer with oil (or garlic oil).

10. Tapioca Wrap Preparation: at this point the tapioca balls should be soft and sticky. Knead the tapioca balls like dough for 1-2 minutes. It should have the foam consistency and be workable like flour dough.

11. Testing: you can test your filling by making one dumpling and steam it. If you find your dumpling too lightly seasoned, add more sugar and fish sauce to the filling.

12. Putting the Dumpling together: have small bowl with room temperature water ready for dipping your fingers into so the tapioca doesn't stick much.

13. Pull a small amount of kneaded tapioca pearls, about the size of the filling ball. Spread the pearls out into a thin layer. Place the filling ball in the middle.

14. Place a finger on the ball while fold your fingers to wrap the tapioca pearls around the filling. Move the pearls from thick spots to cover the whole filling. Squeeze the ball to firm it up .If there is a spot where the filling is exposed, take a very small amount of tapioca pearls and patch the spot.

15. Try to have a uniform wrap that is thick enough to cover the filling, yet still thin enough that it doesn't change the taste and texture.
16. Steaming the ball will cause it to grow larger.
17. Steaming the Dumplings: first, prepare your steamer.
18. Add the dumplings to the steamer. Leave room for expansion, about 1 cm or 1/3 of an inch).
19. Let the dumplings steam for 12-15 minutes, depending on the size of the dumplings. Since the filling is already cooked, you only need to cook the outside tapioca wrap.
20. When the dumplings are cooked, you can see that the tapioca pearls turn transparent. You can see the filling inside. The dumplings appear brownish.
21. When it's cooled, it will give the opaque appearance.
22. Oil the dumplings before removing from the steamer to prevent sticking.
23. Removing the dumplings from the steamer by dipping a spoon into the fried garlic oil to prevent the dumplings from sticking to the spoon.
24. Oil the area on plate where the dumplings will be on with fried garlic oil. Then carefully scoop out the dumplings onto a plate.
25. Add a small amount of the fried garlic with oil on top of each dumpling. Garnish with whole green lettuce, cilantro leaves and fresh Thai chili peppers.
26. Serve warm or room temperature as a snack.
. You can make the tapioca pearl dough ahead of time and keep it in the fridge.

26. Bamboo Shoot recipe

Ingredients:

- 1/2 bottle bamboo shoots
- 1 tsp. fish sauce
- 2 sliced green onion
- 1 tsp. ground dried chili pepper
- 1/2 lime
- 2 tbsp. toasted rice

Method:

1. Slice green onion into 1/4 of an inch.
2. To make toasted rice: toast 2 tablespoons of rice in a pan over low to medium low heat. Keep stirring until the rice turns golden brown about 3 minutes. Remove the toasted rice from the hot pan and let cool. Then grind the rice coarsely.
3. The bamboo shoots for this dish come are a bottle or jar that indicates bamboo shoots in/with Bai Yanang leaves. The juice in the jar is dark green. The shoots are partially shredded. But you will need to shred it all the way through to produce independent strands.
4. Cooking: boil the shredded bamboo shoots in water or its juice. Remove from heat after boiled. Drain the juice and shred the bamboo into small strands.
5. Add sliced green onion, fish sauce, ground dried chili pepper, lime juice and half of ground toasted rice.
6. Mix well and place on a serving plate.
7. Sprinkle the rest of the ground toasted rice.
8. Add more chili pepper, if you like it hot. However, if you find it too hot, add more ground toasted rice to tone down the seasonings.

27. Mushroom Tom Yum Soup

Ingredients:

- 2-3 crushed chili peppers
- 5 sprigs chopped cilantro
- 2 tbsp. fish sauce
- 2 kaffir lime leaves
- crushed lemongrass
- 2/3 lime
- 1 tsp Nam Prig Pow
- 1/2 lb Oyster Mushroom
- 2 1/2 cups water

Method:

1. Wash the mushrooms and set them aside.
2. Crush the lemon grass with the back of your knife.
3. Tie the lemon grass into a knot and drop it into a pot of water. Bring the lemon grass broth to a boil then add the oyster mushrooms.
4. Pull the kaffir lime leaves from their middle stems and drop them in the pot.
5. Add Nam Prig Pow, if desired. Turn off the heat.
6. Crush chili peppers and place them in a serving bowl.
7. Add fish sauce and 2/3 of the lime to the bowl.
8. Pour the soup in the bowl. Taste and see if you might want to add more lime or more fish sauce
9. Add the chili paste.
10. Sprinkle with chopped cilantro and serve hot.

28. Chive Dumplings - Gui Chai

Ingredients:

- 1/2 lb. Chinese chives
- 1 cup rice flour
- 1 tbsp. Soy sauce
- 1/4 cup sticky rice flour
- 1/2 - 1/4 cup tapioca flour
- 1/4 cup cooking oil
- 1/2 cups water
- Chive Dumpling Sauce
- 1 tsp. Dark Sweet Soy Sauce
- 1 tsp. Ground fresh chili paste
- 1 tsp. Soy sauce
- 2 tbsp.   sugar
- 2 tbsp.   vinegar

Method:

1. Add all ingredients together.
2. Ground fresh chili paste can be substituted with fresh sliced green chilies. Serve in a sauce bowl.
3. Add rice flour, sticky rice flour and water to a pot over medium heat.
4. Stir constantly to prevent sticking.
5. If the mixture starts to be too sticky to handle, lower the heat.
6. Stir until the mixture turns gluey.
7. Remove from heat and add 1/4 cup of tapioca flour. Set it aside to let it cool.
8. While waiting for the dough to cool down, slice the Chinese chives into 1/2 inch pieces. Heat up 2 teaspoons of oil in a wok or pan over high heat. Add chives and soy sauce. Stir quickly and remove from the heat. Cooking too

long will produce too much water and make it difficult to stuff the dumpling.

9. Knead the dough. Test the dough to see if it is too sticky. If it is too sticky, it will stick to your hand and will be difficult to work with. Add more tapioca flour.

10. Pinch off a small portion and roll it between your palms into a ball (an inch in diameter). Use your thumb and index finger to thin the dough into a flat piece. Put one tablespoon of cooked Chinese chives in the middle, gather the edges and squeeze them together to close the dumpling.

11. Steam the dumpling for 5-7 minutes or until the dough is cooked.

12. Serve with hot chili soy sauce.

13. You can pan fry the dumplings until they are somewhat brown.

29. Green Papaya Salad

Ingredients:

- 5 Cherry Tomatoes
- 2 chili peppers
- 1 1/2 tbsp. fish sauce
- 1 clove garlic
- 6 green beans
- 2 cups shredded green papaya
- 3/4 lime
- 1 1/2 tbsp. Palm Sugar
- 2 tbsp. toasted peanuts

Method:

1. Smash a clove of garlic first in a mortar. Then add green beans and halved cherry tomatoes. Pound a few times just to bruise the beans and get the juice out of the tomatoes.
2. Add chili peppers and crush them just enough to release the hotness.
3. Add the green papaya, toasted peanuts, fish sauce, lime juice and palm sugar.
4. Use a pestle to push the mixture up in the mortar and the spatula to push it down so that the mixture is mixed well.
5. Serve with sticky rice and a sliver of cabbage, green beans and Thai basil.

30. Cucumber Salad

Ingredients:

- 1 sliced cucumber
- 2 tbsp. Fish sauce
- 2 sliced green onion
- 1/2 sliced 1 in inch lengths onion
- 1 tbsp. sugar
- 1/2 sliced tomato
- 2 tbsp. Cooking oil
- 2 tbsp. vinegar

Method:

1. Cut up the veggies and mix everything together.
2. When you taste it, you should be able to taste all three flavors: fish sauce, vinegar and sugar.

31. Rice - Kow Su-ay

Ingredients:

- 1 cup rice - Thai long grain
- 1 1/2 cup   water

Method:

1. Put rice in a pot that is big enough to prevent boil over (over 1 1/2 quart).
2. Rinse rice in cold water to clean it. The ratio of rice to water is usually one to one and a half.
3. Add more water if you like softer rice.

32. Sticky Rice

Ingredients:

- 1 cup Sticky Rice

Method:

1. Soak the sticky rice in enough cold or lukewarm water to cover the rice for at least an hour or even overnight. Take your steamer, put water in the bottom and cover the steam section with cheesecloth or muslin cloth.
2. Pour the sticky rice on the cheesecloth, cover with the lid and put it on the stove on medium to high heat. Ten minutes into it, move the rice around so the top is down close to the steam. The sticky rice should take about a 20 minutes of steaming to cook and will become translucent when done. Take a small bite to see if it is soft and chewy.
3. The Microwave Method: soak the sticky rice for 10 minutes in warm water in a bowl. Soaking the rice is very important. The water level should be just above the rice, which comes out to be 1 cup of rice and a little over 1 cup of water. Cover the bowl with a dish and cook in microwave for at full power 3 minutes. Stir the rice around to move the rice from the top to the bottom. You will notice that some of the rice is translucent or cooked and some still has white center or the uncooked portion.
4. Heat it up again for another 3 minutes.
5. Check and see if it is done.
6. When cooked, all the rice should be translucent.
7. If it needs more cooking, heat up and check every 3 minutes or so. How long it takes to cook depends on your microwave.

33. Thai Vegan Fried Rice

Ingredients:

- 6 cups cooked long-grain rice
- 2 tbsp. vegetable oil
- 3 tbsp. coarsely chopped garlic
- 1 small onion, finely chopped
- 1/2 tsp. fresh ground black pepper
- 6 ounces green beans, diced
- 4 ounces fresh or frozen corn kernels
- 2 tbsp. soy sauce
- 2 tsp. Thai green curry paste

Method:

1. To start with uncooked rice, start with 2 cups raw rice, cook, spread out on a baking pan to cool, and then refrigerate at least 2 hours or overnight.
2. Prepare the garnishes: cut the scallions on a slight diagonal into 1-inch lengths, cut the cucumber into very thin slices, cut the lime into wedges; set aside.
3. Heat a wok or large frying pan over high heat and add the oil.
4. When the oil is very hot and slightly smoking, add the garlic, onion, and black pepper and stir-fry for 2 minutes.
5. Add the green beans and corn and continue to stir-fry for 3 minutes.
6. Add the cold cooked rice and stir-fry for 5 minutes.
7. Add the soy sauce and curry paste and stir-fry for 2 minutes.
8. Garnish with the scallions, cucumber, and lime, and serve hot.

34. Thai-Inspired Truffle Treats

Ingredients:

- 1/2 cup creamy natural peanut butter
- 1/4 cup palm sugar
- 1 T. lime juice
- 1/2 cup dried, shredded, unsweetened coconut (plus more for rolling)
- 2 T. thick coconut milk

Method:

1. Combine all ingredients in a medium mixing bowl and blend until a dough forms.
2. Form into small balls.
3. Roll in additional shredded coconut.

35. Mango Ice Cream

Ingredients:

- Makes 1 large yogurt container-size tub
- 2 fresh ripe mangos
- 1 cup white sugar
- 3 tbsp. coconut milk
- 1 tsp. lemon juice
- 1 small container whipping cream (about 1 cup)

Method:

1. Slice the mangos open and scoop out fruit from the skins. Don't forget to include fruit around the stone. Place the fruit in a food processor or blender.
2. Add the sugar and blend for 1 minute, or until sugar has dissolved.
3. Add the coconut milk and lemon juice, and briefly blitz to combine.
4. Pour the mango puree into a bowl or container while you continue to use your processor/blender. Scape down the sides and bottom with a rubber spatula to remove as much of the puree as possible.
5. Now pour the whipping cream into the processor/blender. Blitz until the cream forms stiff peaks, or is quite stiff.
6. Add the mango puree to the whipped cream and blitz 5-10 seconds, or until you get a good mango-cream consistency.
7. Pour into a large yogurt container or ice cream tub and set in the freezer for at least 6 hours, preferably 8.
8. Serve in bowls, or scoop into ice cream cones. (To make scooping easier, take the sorbet out of the freezer 10 to 15 minutes ahead of time).

36. Coconut Sorbet

Ingredients:

- 1 cup coconut milk
- 2/3 cup sweetened flaked coconut (baking type)
- 16 oz. 500 ml. container whipping cream
- 1/4 cup sugar
- Topping: 1/4 cup sweetened flaked coconut

Method:

1. Place whipping cream in your food processor or blender and blitz until you have thick whipped cream.
2. Add the coconut milk, flaked coconut, and sugar. Pulse to combine.
3. Transfer mixture to a covered container and place in the freezer. Briefly rinse your blender/processor, but keep it nearby.
4. Check the sorbet after 2-3 hours - it should be frozen around the outside, but still soft inside. Transfer it back into your processor/blender and blitz 15-30 seconds, or until smooth. Return to the container and freeze until solid.
5. Remove container 30 minutes before serving (this will allow the dessert to soften enough so you can easily scoop it into balls).
6. To make the topping, simply place sweetened flaked coconut into a frying pay. "Dry-fry" it over medium-high heat, stirring constantly until coconut turns light golden-brown.
7. Transfer immediately to a bowl and let cool until crunchy (1 minute).
8. Sprinkle over your sorbet.

37. Fried Bananas

Ingredients:

- Start with some ripe bananas and frozen spring-roll wrappers (the smaller ones are preferred).

Method:

- Allow wrappers to thaw for 5-10 minutes, then open packet and carefully separate the first wrapper from the pack.
- Begin to wrap banana.
- Bring sides of wrapper inward, then pull up bottom.
- Tuck end under and continue to roll.
- Finish rolling banana and secure end with water.
- Fry bananas until golden brown.
- Remove from oil and drain.
- Enjoy hot fried bananas plain or with Coconut Ice Cream.

59817623R00033

Made in the USA
San Bernardino, CA
07 December 2017